WORKBOOK
FOR

BREAKING THE HABIT OF BEING YOURSELF

HOW TO LOSE YOUR MIND AND CREATE A NEW ONE

By

DR. JOE DISPENZA

Proudly Brought To You By

WRIGHT PUBLISHERS

Table of Contents

How To Use This Workbook

This workbook is a step-by-step guide for anyone who wants to create a new life for themselves. This is a workbook with practical steps, not a book to be read and dropped. It explains the process of change from your old life to a brand new one.

You only need to follow the steps and not skip anyone because that may affect your progress. You will need to repeat some steps and it's advisable that you do this. Pay attention, stay focused, be honest, and be committed to all you're learning to help you memorize your changes.

You will need to go over all that you're learning as many times as you can to help you indoctrinate your new life. Go over everything you learn and practice it daily. You are only as good as the changes you're practicing at each moment.

Remember that the life you've always lived which is your old life is normal to you so it wouldn't be easy for your mind and body to accept this change. Be patient with yourself and follow the changes no matter how boring it seems.

INTRODUCTION

Breaking the habit of being yourself by Dr Joe Dispenza is focused on stepping out of the old mind with the thoughts that come from that mind with the emotions that are linked to your body in that state.

When you step out of this to your new self, you'll notice that you're tougher than you believe and you're more powerful than you've ever known.

With this book, you'll see that your thoughts are powerful, and they have a lasting effect on you. You'll be able to intentionally move into a state of consciousness that makes you link to your universal intelligence, you can make contact with the array of possibilities that lie before you and send clear signals that make us expectant for change. You'll receive feedback to assure you that this change is happening.

You find a couple of strategies that will help you reprogram your subconscious so your nerve cells can unfire and unwire to fire and wire anew. This will help you to change your thoughts, change your feelings so your brain and body are created anew, and produce a new you.

Who is it for?
This workbook is for anyone who wants to break from themselves. If you're tired of your old way of life or the old patterns you subconsciously live by, then this book is for you.

What's in it and why is it important to me?
With this book, you can be sure that your life will be better. You will love yourself and you can live above every survival emotion that you've always relied on.

You'll notice an improvement in the way you think and feel and the things you've assigned to your personality can be changed because they aren't the real you. You can make changes from your subconscious as you gain control of your mind, your body, and your life. You'll live above destructive negative feelings and get into a new state of being.

This book is the way to attain your true self. You may get bored when you follow the steps mentioned in the book but it's a good thing because it shows you're beginning to learn the steps. In a short while, you'll find yourself in the right state of being, living, and loving your life.

CHAPTER SUBDIVISIONS

Each chapter has six subdivisions.

1. Summary: the summary tells you what to expect in the chapter.

2. Key takeaways: this is what you learn in this chapter.

3. Lessons: these are life nuggets to help you with different aspects of your life.

4. Goals: the focus of the chapter

5. Action plans: how the goals will be accomplished

6. Questions: this tests your knowledge of this chapter.

Part I: THE SCIENCE OF YOU

CHAPTER ONE: THE QUANTUM YOU

Summary

Your mind is a powerful tool. It shapes our thoughts, perceptions, and worldview. This implies that any form of change will begin in your mind. The way we think and the decisions we make are a result of what we choose to believe.

Change is difficult because you've lived in a particular way for a long time. You've been schooled properly in that way. Sometimes when you think of change, your mind hasn't left the previous way it used to work which makes change impossible.

Many people have come up with theories to help us understand the mind and its link to matter. Rene Descartes proposed that the universe was governed by predictable laws. He believed the mind had so many variables that would make it impossible for it to fit into any objective laws of the physical world. Matter was limited to the world of science while the mind was God's instrument and was to be left in the coffers of religion. To him and Isaac Newton, human beings can't determine their outcomes because reality is predetermined, and humans are victims since we can't control actions.

To Einstein, the parts of the observable physical world are both particles (physical matter) and waves (energy) depending on the observer. He noticed that matter doesn't always behave in predictable ways.

In the quantum realm, there's a reality in which you're happy, and healthy, and you have all you need with the capacity for it that you hold in your mind and thoughts.

There are two types of consciousness. There's an objective part that relates to life intelligently. There's also the subjective part that is self-aware and free-willed.

Key takeaways from this chapter

- Our mind is what shapes our reality. How your life turns out is a product of what you believe. When you look at yourself through the mirror, you only see what you believe not what you're looking at.

- When you create new constructive thoughts, you'll see and enjoy a new you.

- You may wonder why you can't have true and lasting change as every change you experience is fleeting and transitory. This is because you haven't overhauled your mind and thought processes about the way things happen.

- A particle can't be seen in reality until the observer focuses on the location. An observer will influence the behavior of time and energy. This is called the observer effect. This helped to prove that matter and mind didn't need to be separated. This established the fact that the mind, as subjective as it was, could influence the objective, physical world.

- On the subatomic level, energy responds to what the mind pays attention to for it to become matter.

- Everything in the physical world consists of electrons which are subatomic particles. These particles exist as potential, and they are in a wave state when no one pays attention to them. They are all around and nowhere until it is observed.

- If your mind affects the presence of an electron, then it can affect the appearance of any possibility. You can shape matter because you are energy with consciousness.

- The quantum world lies with an array of possibilities. All that it needs to come into reality is an observer (you) that will influence energy in the form of potential matter with the consciousness or mind to create waves of energetic probabilities merged into physical matter.

- When there's an intentional thought, there must be an energizer which is an elevated emotion.

- You can't change your life without changing your energy because your energy is what brings an elemental change in your emotions and mind.

- Our thoughts are like waves. They can be straight or wavy, coherent, or incoherent. When you have a focused, clear, and aligned thought about what you want to achieve, you send a strong electromagnetic signal that brings you closer to the reality you desire.

- When there's no collaboration between the mind and body, then change remains a potential.

- Gratitude is important because it helps you feel whatever you want in the future as if you've had it.

- Change happens when we hold firmly to the belief that by choosing the signal to send out or the thought to hold, we will get an unexpected yet observable effect.
- When expecting change, the last thing we will experience is a sensory feedback. Let go of all you see or feel around you, stay unaware of your body, and forget about time.

Lessons

- Nobody is perfect.
- If you don't see yourself in a new way, change will be impossible.
- You become what you think.
- Focus on what you want and not your problems or what you don't have.
- You can't hold on to previous beliefs and expect change to happen.
- If you pay attention to what you want even if you can't see it, you'll get it.
- The mind can influence matter. When your mind and body are one, it will influence your external world.
- You don't have to direct how future events unfold in your life. Sometimes you need to learn how to surrender, trust and let go and see how the event plays out.
- To change your life, you need to change your mind.

Goals

- To understand why quantum outcomes must be a surprise.
- To learn to give thanks for a future event.
- To have dominion over your environment, your body, and time.

- To overcome your senses
- To cause an effect

Action plans

- Understanding quantum outcomes and why it must be a surprise.
- Learning gratitude
- Taking control over your environment, body, and time
- Overcoming your senses
- Causing an effect

Questions

1. How important are your thoughts?
2. Is it possible to create a new reality? If your answer is yes, how?
3. How can you create lasting change?
4. Do you believe your thoughts shape your destiny? Explain the reason for your answer.
5. Can paying attention to anything you want change your life?
6. How can change happen in life?
7. Can going Newtonian affect your ability to create? Explain the reason for your answer.
8. Why is it important to give thanks and have elevated emotions about an event before it happens?
9. Your nephew comes home from a job interview. He is sad because he didn't pass the interview even though he qualified for the job. He tells you this happens to him every time and he thinks he's cursed. Tell him what he's doing wrong and how to change it.

CHAPTER TWO: OVERCOMING YOUR ENVIRONMENT

Summary

Your mind is the key to the world. In this chapter, you'll see that your thoughts can create your reality. it can create an alternative reality from the cycle and mental map that your mind follows. If you keep thinking about your familiar thoughts and feelings, you will have the same reality that you had in your past. Nothing will change. But if you're going to get the change you need, you must be ready for something different. You must change your routine, your thought processes, and everything about you.

There are three important elements that are important when it comes to change. They are time, your body, and your energy. You must be bigger than these three.

The brain is a seat of action. It is from the brain that our actions emanate. It processes all the knowledge that comes to it and these informations are the things it has been open to from your environment. When your brain is trained to follow the traditions you've created for it in your personal reality, it will stick to it. It is called Hebb's law.

Key takeaways from this chapter

- As an observer, there's power in your hands. You can influence the subatomic realm and affect any event by reducing a single electron from a wave of energy into a particle.
- With your consciousness, you can influence the realm of atoms since its components are made from energy and consciousness.

- When you stick with your daily routine, you will create the same circumstances, experience the same feelings, and get the same predictable outcomes. When you focus on your problems, you will be creating the same web of problems for yourself.

- If you focus on your environment, time, and your body and you think equally to them, you can't be bigger than the situations you find yourself and you wouldn't live above your problems. To break these cycles, you must be bigger. Be bigger than the situations that happen to you, be bigger than the emotions stored in your mind and body, and live within a different line of time.

- The brain keeps a record of all your experiences, and knowledge you acquired from the environment whether consciously or subconsciously. This information is saved in the synaptic connections of the brain. This information covers the things you're conversant with, your relationships with different people, the things you have, the different people you met at specific places and your bond with them, the different places you lived, or you've been to, the experiences you gained at different places and the connection you have with different places.

- The brain creates a network of nerve cells from your experiences with people from specific places and at particular times which is what creates your external environment.

- Your brain isn't just a record of your environment. It is equal to your environment because of the records of your past and your life generally. This means you'll think and act according to your environment. This is why you are a product of what you think. Your internal thoughts will be equal to your external life.

- Changing your life begins with changing your personality. It is changing the way you feel, think, and act. This means a complete change to who you are.

- A powerful individual is one whose behaviors and intentions match, whose mind and body are in sync, and whose actions and thoughts are equal.

- People who have been known to be great individuals throughout history are those who are:

  o Unapologetically devoted to their future destiny and they see no need to receive feedback from their environment.

  o They constantly reminded themselves of the future they wanted for themselves

  o Their minds were far beyond their environment because they couldn't afford to let their environment control their thoughts. They knew what they wanted to happen

  o The thoughts, emotions, and actions they had and carried out were not realistic to others around them.

- The four elements used to change the brain are repetition, learning knowledge, paying attention, and receiving hands-on instruction.

- When you think about something and forget everything else, you'll eventually experience the thought.

Lessons

- Your mind has a real and lasting effect on your life.
- We all need models we can emulate.

- Your internal thoughts and external life are the same because your reality is what conditions your thoughts and emotions.
- With familiar memories, you can only recreate the same experiences and outcomes.
- Your environment is the controller of your mind, and your mind is a result of your consciousness.
- Living by a routine can keep you locked in the past. This means you may can live your life on autopilot.
- The power to end a cycle lies in your hands.
- With mental rehearsal, you can outgrow repetitive cycles. Mental rehearsal is used to replace old cycles with new ones.

Goals
- To be bigger than your environment, time, and your body
- To practice mental rehearsal
- To prevent your environment from conditioning your future
- To break out of cycles
- To practice the four elements that can help you change your brain.

Action plans
- Becoming bigger than your environment, time, and your body
- Practicing mental rehearsal
- Preventing your environment from conditioning your future
- Breaking out of cycles
- Practicing the four elements that can help you change your brain.

Questions
1. What can you gain when you continue with daily repetitive cycles?

2. Why do you need a model if you want to change?

3. Is it possible for a person to keep thinking in the past without knowing? Can your past become your future? Explain the reason for your answer.

4. What are the four elements needed to change the brain and how do they work?

CHAPTER THREE: OVERCOMING YOUR BODY

Summary

The brain is a powerhouse. Every time you need to do something, it begins in the brain. Your thoughts start in the brain, and it begins with you making a chemical and a biochemical reaction in the brain. After this, the brain sends certain chemical signals (which are the messengers of that thought) to the body. The body receives this thought and obeys it immediately by ushering in the right set of reactions to align with the thought from the brain. The body responds to this thought immediately by sending a message to the brain to attest that its feelings are aligned with the brain's thoughts.

You can live out an event in your past more than a thousand times. The body stores the emotion linked to the event and it triggers that thought whenever it thinks of it.

A personality is totally formed when a person is in their mid-30s. This means people who have passed their mid-30s have properly learned by heart the set of attitudes, skills, beliefs, behaviors, associated memories, emotional reactions, perceptions, and habits that work within them and control them because all of these make up the mind. 5 percent of the mind is conscious, and the rest runs on autopilot.

If your reference is the feelings from your past, you wouldn't be able to live outside your past.

Key takeaways from this chapter

- The body has cells with a receptor site on their exteriors that receive information from outside their boundaries. The cells are initiated to carry out certain tasks when there is a match in the frequency, chemistry, and electrical charge between the signal coming in from outside and the receptor site.

- When there are neuropeptides, neurotransmitters, and hormones, they are the cause-and-effect chemical for the activities in the brain and the body's functioning. These three are ligands.

- Neurotransmitters are chemical messengers in charge of sending signals between nerve cells and they allow the brain and nervous system to interact. They inform a neuron to detach from its present connection and attach better to its present connection. They switch the message that's sent to a neuron and rewrite it, so a different message is sent to the connected nerve cells. They send chemical messages from the brain and mind.

- When there are messages that need to be passed between the brain and body, you'll find neuropeptides. They are mainly messengers. They are created in the hypothalamus, and they move through the pituitary gland which releases a chemical message to the body with certain instructions. They enter the bloodstream, attach to glands, and then they initiate hormones that influence us to have certain feelings. They are a link between the brain and body to enable us to feel what we think.

- Hormones are chemicals linked to feelings.

- When you have uplifting and happy thoughts, your brain produces chemicals that make you feel what you think. If you are feeling down or sad, you produce chemicals that make you feel sad or depressed.

- When you feel the way you think, and think the way you feel, it creates a cycle and a feedback loop known as a state of being.

- When you ponder on a highly charged emotional event that happened to you, you make the brain create the exact sequences and pattern when that event happened to you, making your brain to recreate your past by fixing itself on the past which strengthens the circuits into more hardwired networks. It doesn't stop there. The same chemicals that were released when the event happened will be released again and it's almost as if the event is happening physically again. The chemicals make sure the body learns to memorize the emotion. The chemical result of thinking and feeling as well as feeling and thinking and the neurons linking and working together train the mind into a fixed set of automatic curricula.

- When your body remembers an emotion too well, better than a conscious mind, the body becomes the mind in this scenario and a habit is formed.

- When we reach the age of 35, we become a set of involuntary programs, habitual emotional response, and memorized behavior for 95 percent of each day.

- When the mind comes awake and tries to regain control, the body launches into defense mode. It talks us out of our conscious goals, reminding us of every time we tried and failed. It reminds us of our shortcomings and how we've always failed every time we attempted to step into our conscious goals.

- As long as you use feelings you're comfortable with as a benchmark for feedback, you'll not be able to reach out for greatness and grow bigger than the environment within.

- If you're going to break habits, then you'll need to investigate your physical health. Genes are not the basic cause of diseases. When you change your feelings, thoughts, and emotional reactions, and you make healthier choices as regards your lifestyle, your cells will get new signals and they can express new proteins without changing their genetic blueprint. When you think and feel the same way and you stick with familiar states of being, your chemical state will activate the same genes which means you make the same proteins and your body doesn't produce anything different.

Lessons

- The way you think is what conditions your body.
- Your emotions or feelings shouldn't be the way you think.
- We only appear to be awake almost throughout the day.
- Learn to reach out for new feelings to help you break out of your old cycle.
- Your feelings and thoughts are more powerful than you know or choose to believe.
- Your operating system isn't conscious of only negative emotions. It's just conscious of what you have given to it frequently. It can also learn what you want it to learn.
- Feelings and emotions are the products of our experiences.

- Changing your state of being is what you need to change your personality.
- Some genes are more open to change than others.
- Emotions alone can create a thought.

Goals
- To understand how the brain works.
- To get a new mind
- To condition your body with a new mind
- To recreate yourself
- To break the habit of yourself by rejecting the body's desire to continue the unhealthy old order.
- To unlearn your feelings
- To recondition your body to a new mind

Action plans
- Understanding the way the brain functions.
- Getting a new mind
- Conditioning your body with a new mind
- Recreating yourself
- Breaking the habit of yourself and rejecting the body's desire to continue the unhealthy old order.
- Unmemorizing your feelings
- Reconditioning your body to a new mind.

Questions
1. As the thought is to the brain, so are feelings to _____?
2. What does it mean to be in a state of being?

3. How does a state of being, affect your reality?

4. How can the body drive the mind? Is it the same thing as the mind controlling the body? Explain the difference.

5. What is the greatest habit we need to break?

6. What happens when your mind becomes conscious and tries to take control?

7. What are the downsides of memorized feelings?

8. What is the genetic impact of sticking to a routine?

CHAPTER FOUR: OVERCOMING TIME

Summary

Memorizing an emotion begins with you thinking about a thought and it produces a memory. The memory in turn creates an emotion. Give it some time and this thought becomes a memory and an emotion is linked to it. With continuous repetition, the thought and the memory are the same which becomes an emotion. Eventually, we memorize the emotion.

Moods and temperaments are linked but they are not the same. A mood can lead to a temperament. Both mood and temperament are different from personality traits although they both lead to a personality trait.

When you want to change your personality, you must step out of the personality that you've memorized. You may identify some traits as your personality when in actual sense, it isn't your personality, but you're simply attached to the past. When your body has been trained to take the place of your mind, you're in a predictable future and you are living from the past.

To get over autopilot and ingrained habits, you need to live higher than time.

Remember that you have the power to create a new you. Don't obsessively focus on a stressful event in your future because of a similar experience in your past. Instead, think about a new desirable experience that awaits you and embrace it. Focus on it and embrace it emotionally. This way, you'll find that you'll begin to experience the high-end emotions linked to that experience in the present. You don't have to be special to do this, because you already have the neurological ability to make it happen.

Key takeaways from this chapter

- By staying in the present, you can move beyond the boundaries of time and space and bring potential into reality. But when you opt to stay in the past, none of those potentials can come to life.

- When we try to change, we behave like addicts who are stuck in a particular chemical state of being.

- With the aid of memories, the body can act like the mind. It only needs to recall an emotionally charged experience and then you think about it. This thought becomes a memory that brings back the emotions linked to that experience. As you stay with that memory consistently, your emotions, memory, and thoughts become one and you will memorize this feeling. This means you can easily stay in the past whether you know it or not.

- The subconscious or autonomic nervous system is made up of mental and physical processes that happen without our consciousness. It is in charge of making sure the body is functioning. Some of these processes are breathing in and out, maintaining the body temperature, blinking your eyes, keeping the heart beating, and other processes.

- A conditioned response is what your body expects because it has associated a particular act with an event over time.

- We need to step out of emotional addictions to events from the past because this will draw us away from the present and back into the past.

- Moods linger for a while. This is because it is a chemical state of being which is usually short-term as a result of an extended emotional reaction. It is set off by something in your environment, aided by a few minor annoying issues which incite an emotional reaction from you. The chemicals produced by this reaction don't fizzle out immediately, they linger for a while till the effect wears off. If it takes some hours to days for it to wear off, then it's a mood.

- When you stay in a mood, and things constantly make you upset or remind you that you're upset, you're no longer experiencing a mood but a temperament. When temperaments linger for years, it becomes a personality. Personality traits are who we are, how we act or react, and what we think and feel can be linked to events from the past.

- When you condition yourself to live from the future, you decide to live consciously and live for the better by deliberately focusing on a new and desirable experience. You begin to experience the emotion of an event before it happens, and the body acts accordingly by living as if the event is happening. This can be a negative emotion and experience or a positive one. If it is a negative emotion and experience, you rob yourself of the idea of a beautiful future outcome in any event.

- When you live in the flow, everything in your environment, body, and your sense of timing is suspended. You feel peace from within because you're at ease and relaxed and you're in a conscious state.

Lessons
- Staying in the present is more challenging than it sounds.
- Change is one of the constant things in life, but human beings don't like to change.

- Sometimes we may feel that we are in the present, but we are stuck in the past because our minds, thoughts, and emotions are deeply rooted in the past.
- Our personality traits are born out of the past.
- You can train your body to live in the present and future.
- Becoming bigger than the Big Three is living in the flow.

Goals
- To change your personality
- To move out of the past
- To unmemorize emotions.
- To live in the present
- To be greater than the big three

Action plans
- Changing your personality
- Moving out of the past
- Unmemoraizing emotions
- Living in the present
- Becoming greater than the big three

Questions
1. How do we memorize emotions?
2. Can the autonomic nervous system be described as autopilot? Explain the reason for your answer.
3. Why is it so hard to change?
4. What's the difference between a mood and a temperament?
5. How can you live in the future?
6. What do you gain when you live in the future?

CHAPTER FIVE: SURVIVAL VS CREATION

Summary

There's a survival mode and creation mode for all humans. It's either you live in survival mode, or you live in creation mode as you can't live in both worlds. There are things we do that keep us there just as there are things, we can do to take us out of it. By living in the past, you're staying in stress and survival mode.

The difference between animals and humans experiencing stress is that humans can live and relive stressful or traumatic events. When this happens constantly, it becomes a norm. This can lead to the dysregulation of some of our genes which may lead to diseases.

The threat that turns on the fight-flight mode can be real or perceived. The fight-flight mode provides a huge jolt of energy, waking up our bodies and parts of the brain for a short while as the Big Three gets all the attention. However, this 'short while' is fleeting.

We can change ourselves. We have the frontal lobe which houses the prefrontal cortex with the capacity and functions that are strong enough to bring about the change we desire. It can shut down the attention that the Big Three demand from you.

Key takeaways from this chapter

- When we feel that we are in danger, our sympathetic nervous system is initiated, and energy is mobilized to do what we need to keep us safe. According to history, this is what we use to confront threats from prey and other things that serve as a risk to our survival.

- Stress is what pushes the body out of its chemical balance. The stress response is the body's natural response when it is put out of balance and what it does to get back to equilibrium.

- As humans, we can use our thoughts to turn on the fight or flight mode (which is what gets turned on when we feel stressed). This thought may not be something in your present, it can be something from your future. It may be turned on because of something you're anticipating in the future or from something that happened to you when you were younger. You can anticipate stress-response-producing-experiences or you can recollect them. You can turn short-term stressful events into long-term situations.

- When you're constantly stressed and you don't turn off the fight-flight response, you'll break down eventually. With your fight-flight response constantly turned on without being turned off, your heart will keep racing which means you may have high blood pressure, arrhythmias, or other health challenges. This is because you're focusing all your energy on what's happening around you externally and you have no strength to do anything creative internally. This will affect your immune system which serves as the defense of your internal system and this can make you prone to illnesses and diseases. Fight or flight mode uses up the energy of your internal environment.

- When you constantly overproduce stress hormones, it leads to an internal environment of depression, fear, frustration, envy, anger, sadness, aggression, hatred, insecurity, suffering, anxiety, worry, and hopelessness.

- When we live in survival mode, we focus on the Big Three. The hormones and stress response it triggers make us obsess about time, our body, and the environment. The effect of this is that we become materialistic we are only conscious of our external environment. We lose our identity as it becomes lost inside us since we only focus on the outward. We are detached from the universal field of intelligence.

- When we don't know how to focus on ourselves and come out of survival mode, we focus on the .00001 percent, and we are oblivious to the fact that 99.9999 percent exists. By only staying physically present, we'll think like physical beings, not as beings of energy. We become more of matter and less of mind.

- Higher frequency emotions such as gratitude, joy, peace, and love fill an individual with more energy and reduce physical or material attributes. Low-frequency emotions such as guilt, hatred, frustration, anxiety, suffering, worry, shame, and suffering makes an individual more physical or material and less of mind.

- When we focus on the Big Three due to stress, we unconsciously crave our problems, our lows, or unhealthy relationships. We keep these situations close to fuel our addiction to these situations as it reminds us that we are somebody; plus, we enjoy the jolt of energy it brings. With our thoughts constantly going back to this, we keep negative energy around us.

- In a normal survival mode emergency, the self is the most important thing. But when the body is under long-term stress, chemicals move the brain and body out of balance making sure the self is constantly the most important thing which makes an individual constantly selfish.
- If we use our senses to define our reality, this reality (from our senses) will be the law that governs us.
- When we stay in creation and not survival, we initiate the frontal lobe which consists of the prefrontal cortex. This part is the head of the brain's creative center and the seat of decision-making. It oversees consciousness, concentration, awareness, and attention. It controls impulsive and emotional behavior and allows us to learn new things.

Lessons
- Your thoughts are one of the most powerful tools you have.
- You may constantly experience negative circumstances because you're expecting stress or reliving it through memory.
- The three most important things we focus on when our stress response is triggered are the body, time, and the environment.
- When you're only in touch with your physical reality, you'll end up trying to control your reality instead of surrendering to something greater.
- Survival mode breeds self-centeredness
- If your thoughts can be the reason why you have health challenges, it can also be the reason why your health will improve.

- To live in creation means you live as a nobody but living in survival makes you live as a somebody.

- You need to be aware of your old self to become more conscious and embrace a new life.

- Metacognition is the means of transporting you from the past to a new future.

Goals

- To step out of survival mode
- To see reasons why you shouldn't focus on the Big Three.
- To live as a nobody
- To use your metacognitive abilities to modify yourself.

Action plans

- Living free of survival mode
- Living out of the Big Three
- Living as a nobody
- Using your metacognitive abilities to modify yourself.

Questions

1. Mention some things you do that can keep you in survival mode.
2. Why is repetitive stress harmful to humans?
3. What happens when you spend so much time on negative thoughts and feelings?
4. What are the benefits of living as a nobody?
5. What are the three essential functions of the frontal lobe?

PART II: YOUR BRAIN AND MEDITATION

CHAPTER SIX: THREE BRAINS: THINKING TO DOING TO BEING

Summary

As you gain more understanding about your brain, you can utilize its functions and use meditative process to improve your life.

Changing your life isn't instantaneous. It is a process with different steps. It begins manually or mechanically and then it becomes automatic. It's like driving. As an amateur driver, you begin by becoming too conscious and you pay attention to everything you did because you had to think of what you wanted to do, then you did it. When you became better, you did it without thinking about it and your subconscious mind eventually became the driver (that's what usually happens) so driving is automatic to you.

When you think of the change you want, you create new neurological connections and circuits to showcase your new thoughts. That's why thinking is the first step to change. The brain is open to new experiences and learning. Pruning and sprouting (which can also be called unlearning and learning) gives us the ability to rise higher than our present hindrances and be greater than the situations we find ourselves.

Key takeaways from this chapter

- The progression the brain follows to facilitate learning is thinking, doing, and being respectively. However, its possible to skip doing and move from thinking to being. You can think about who you want to be and be who you want to be.

- The brain is excited when it's time to learn new things. It examines, identifies, analyzes, extrapolates classifies, and sorts the information it receives in the way you need it.

- To understand how you can change your mind, you need to be conversant with the concept of hardwiring which is the process of how neurons participate in long-term, habitual relationships. This is why nerve cells that work together also connect and nerve cells that don't work together disconnect. This is why it is possible to let go of beliefs and thought processes that you don't want to live by anymore.

- To change your life, you must begin by changing your feelings and thoughts and then take action that aligns with the new thought and feelings. This will produce a new feeling that the body will memorize till we get into a state where the mind and body align (state of being).

- The three brains that help with change are the neocortex (which is the thinking brain), the limbic brain (which creates, maintains, and sorts the chemicals in the body), and the cerebellum (which is the realm of the subconscious mind.

- The neocortex is tasked with learning, remembering, analyzing, planning, creating, building, reasoning, speculating, and interacting. It processes what you see and hear and helps you connect with your external reality. It helps you understand the information you receive but haven't experienced so that you can easily accept this in the future when knowledge and experience meet. With the help of the neocortex, you can adjust your behavior and attitude so you can do things differently and have a different outcome when the opportunity for this comes.

- The limbic brain is the highest-developed part of the brain in humans, dolphins, and mammals. It helps to create long-term memories because there are emotions that attach to memories.

- The cerebellum helps to memorize actions, attitudes, behavior, and emotional reaction until it becomes a state of being. It stores information about simple actions, emotional reactions, deeply ingrained attitudes, conditioned behaviors, unconscious reflexes, and skills that are stored up in the memory. Once you've done something so much and for so long, it stores this information.

- When you give up your old thought patterns and you intrude on emotional reactions that have become a habit and let go of previous behaviors and plan new ways of being, you're acting out the thought in you and the knowledge you've acquired so you can create a new mind. This is how to tell yourself about the person you want to be.

- When you put yourself into an experience before it happens, you're rewiring your neural circuitry to think like the event has taken place. The neural networks will begin to connect and your brain creates a picture, a model, or a hologram of the ideal self you want to focus on. This becomes real to you and the brain upscales this experience to seem like it has happened.

- To master a thing is to get your internal chemical state to become bigger than anything in the external world.

- The brain has two memory systems which are the explicit memories and implicit memories. The explicit or declarative memories can declare what has been learned from semantic memories or episodic experiences. Episodic memories keep a longer imprint than sensory memories. Implicit or non-declarative memories keep record of things that have become second nature to us.

- When we apply what we learn intellectually, we change our behavior in a way. repeating this action easily will move it to a state of being (the cerebellum is in control).

- You can create a state of being without having a corresponding experience.

- With meditation, you can change your thoughts, your brain, your body, and your state of being without physical action.

Lessons

- The first step to change is your thoughts. If you can think it, you can change it.

- Knowledge is for the mind and experience is for the body.

- Without experience, knowledge is not different from philosophy.

- Without knowledge, experience is ignorance.

- If you can master a negative emotion, you can master a positive one.

- Wisdom is knowledge that has been gathered through continuous experience.

Goals

- To understand your brain and how it functions
- To maximize the use of your brain
- To be conscious of your unconscious self

Action plans

- Understanding your brain and its functions
- Maximizing the brain usage
- Becoming conscious of your unconscious self

Questions

1. What is the key to quantum creating?
2. Why is the brain important to change?
3. What are the benefits of neuroplasticity?
4. What are the different functions of the three brains?
5. Why is knowledge important to your mind?
6. Is it possible to move from thinking to being without taking any corresponding action?
7. How do you know when you've become a master?
8. Why is meditation important? What are the benefits of meditation?
9. How can you know when meditation has stimulated your three brains to get the required result?

CHAPTER SEVEN: THE GAP

Summary

What you regard as pleasure or happiness may be nothing but a reaction to stimuli from the material world and it's easier to get addicted to it. Most times we live in two separate entities by having a separate projection when we are with others and another for who we really are. For everyone, there are different layers of emotion that we commit to memory from our past experiences that create the gap between who we are and who we want others to see.

When people get hooked or addicted to something, they believe it will silence the internal crisis. If it makes you feel good and pleasurable, you choose it above other things. The more you pour yourself into it to take away what you feel, the more committed you will need to be the next time you're doing it.

Relationships are built with people you can connect with. They remind you of something from the past or they can connect to the picture of your future. You can build emotional memories with them. You share the same energy and you can build bonds from it.

Key takeaways from this chapter

- Happiness comes from who you are not what you do.
- Many people are overdependent and over-immersed in their external environment and they get their approval from it. They fill their emotional bank from it and live from there. The downside is that they feel empty when they are alone, or they will be unable to

live with themselves. To manage this, people use separate entities: one for how we appear and the other for who we really are.

- How we appear is a disguise or acting. It is what we put up or a carved identity we want people to interact with. It is our facade personality which depends on externalities to help it identify as somebody. It will do everything to hide itself and push away the feelings of emptiness that exists when we are alone. We start putting up this mask right from when we are younger, and we use it to hide our insecurities.

- Who we really are is the way we feel when all externalities are out of the way, and we are with ourselves. We hide this part of ourselves from others. If you want to know what this is, sit with yourself and don't get distracted by your phone, people, or things. It is what you feel when you fail, the anger that wells up within, feelings of frustration, shame, guilt, what you worry about, and the reason behind your anxiety.

- To remind ourselves of who we think we are, we refabricate our experiences to validate our personality.

- From a young age, we have identified ourselves by and with emotionally charged events. Whenever we replay or relieve these experiences mentally, the body also does the same. We keep this running till it becomes a mood, then a temperament, and eventually a personality.

- By midlife, all our personality is fully formed, and we are aware of what to expect from our experiences because we have an idea of everything that comes our way. We've lived in the routine and know what life is all about. The new experiences have been experienced by thought and we can predict the feelings that come with it. By midlife, there's nothing new happening. This means nothing can take away the hollow within. This is what people refer to as midlife crisis. The environment and external world can't affect the emptiness anymore. This is when some people engage in other activities or change locations, get a plastic surgery, pick up a challenging course, or make new friends. Some others engage in extreme actions such as substance abuse or commit suicide.

- If you opt for diverting what you feel within, you'll become dependent on externalities to distract you from what's going on within. This will make you go deeper into a bottomless pit as you focus on other externalities to keep the empty feeling at bay. However, you'll notice later that you need a double or triple effect to keep the feelings away and avoid the pain it brings.

- When you ask yourself pertinent questions such as who I am, what is God, what is my purpose in life, what really makes me happy, who do I love, is there more to life, you'll find out that your soul will begin to come alive.

- When you create bonds with people, your energy is connected to theirs. To step out of the emotion you've memorized and unmask who you are, and your energy to do this. This is why emotions are described as energy in motion.

- It takes energy to break bonds with people you're connected with.

- Addictions are fueled by a memorized emotion. You can't resolve your problems if you're still hooked on to the issues in the past and analyzing them at the same time. To get over it, you need to forget about self-limiting emotions.

Lessons

- It's easy to get carried away with what you do and not remember who you are.
- There must be an alignment between your inner self and your outer projection.
- Your identity can be born from various emotions.
- We have all been scarred in one way from traumatic experiences as young people.
- Many of the things you do or attribute to your personality reflect the feelings you're trying to avoid from earlier in life.
- The more you buy and consume things to keep who you really are hidden, the louder who you really are becomes.
- No external distraction can serve as an answer to what you feel within.
- Self-reflection makes the soul come alive.
- If you had an experience that made you seem weak or insecure when you were a child and you still feel that way as an adult, then you stopped growing emotionally as a child and you didn't see your experience as a lesson to be learned.
- Pleasure doesn't bring true happiness.
- Wisdom is memory without its emotional strength.
- If you don't step out of the past, you will never see your future.

Goals

- To unmask who we want people to think we are.
- To bridge the gap between who we want people to think we are and who we really are.
- To see your true personality
- To understand what keeps you busy.
- To see your experiences as a lesson
- To unmemorize emotions that form your identity.
- To break the bonds of emotional addiction
- To see the benefit of meditation

Action plans

- Unmasking who we want people to think we are.
- Closing the gap between our dual personalities
- Seeing your true personality
- Understanding what keeps you busy.
- Turning experiences into lessons.
- Unmemorizing emotions that are a part of your identity.
- Breaking the bonds of emotional addiction
- Benefiting from meditation

Questions

1. Why do people run from the emptiness within?
2. What can you do to confront the hollowness within?

CHAPTER EIGHT: MEDIATION, DEMYSTIFYING THE MYSTICAL, AND WAVES OF YOUR FUTURE

Summary

To become vigilant, to step out of your emotional bonds with your body, time, and environment, and to close the gap, you need meditation. With meditation, you are no longer subconscious, but you consciously use your will to take control of your emotions, beliefs, thought processes, and actions so you break the chains and be free to be your new self. With meditation, you can make the change you want, and this is possible because you can do this with the help of your frontal lobe.

When you take away stimuli from your material world by shutting your eyes and senses to everything around you so that you go quiet and still, you wouldn't get carried away by time. You will be aware of the thoughts and feelings running through your mind and body. You will see that you can focus on your unconscious states of mind and body, and you will be familiar with yourself and the things you do unconsciously until you become conscious of your thoughts. This can only happen when you meditate.

When you meditate, you can open the pathway that exists between the conscious and subconscious mind. You can enter the operating system of your subconscious. This means you can identify the habits and attitudes that aren't helpful on the journey to find your new self and make the changes you need. With meditation, you move from the Beta waves through the Alpha waves to the Theta wave state which is where you need to be

Key takeaways from this chapter

- One important way you can break free of yourself is to be alert, which you can do by observing your thoughts (becoming more metacognitive) or staying still, monitoring your behavior, and understanding how your environment instigates your emotional reactions.

- When you meditate, you can get into the operating mechanism of your subconscious mind. This will allow you to step out from yourself, your thoughts, emotions, actions, and beliefs so you can watch these things and then you can subconsciously reprogram your body and brain to a new mind.

- The most important aspect of making change is to observe yourself. It is you moving from doing everything to watching more and doing less. This is because you can't switch from your old to your new life if you don't know the difference between the two. To step out of the old self, you need to know what the old self is just as you need to know what the new self is. It is only with observation that you can see this clearly.

- When you focus on your thought so much that it literally becomes something you experience, it will create an emotion. This emotion is what you need to feel for your new self. As these feelings start to become familiar, you will associate them with your new identity and present reality. This is how you move beyond time and move into a state of being. When you repeat this process consistently, it will become automatic in a little while.

- To be sure you're stepping into a future with your new self, you must clear away the weeds in your mind so you can plant new seeds of thoughts, emotions, and behavior for your new self. To cultivate the new seeds demands that you take conscious steps to plant, take out weeds, and water every good thing. As you do this, you're putting yourself in control so that nothing grows on its own.

- To change, you must unlearn. This involves the trimming of circuits. Change also involves learning which involves the firing and wiring of your brain. This will prevent any old thoughts that try to take control of your mind.

- Human beings have a wide range of brain states, from delta waves (which is a low-level activity state when we are asleep) to the alpha waves (the creative and imaginative state), to the theta waves (a state between deep sleep and being awake), the beta waves (state of conscious thought) and Gamma waves (high-frequency state).

- The beta waves are further divided into three levels which are the low-range, mid-range, and high-range. The high-range beta is activated during emergencies, stress, and fight-flight mode. In this state, the brain is overfocused and concentrated and this state doesn't allow the mind or body to be in order. This means staying in this state for too long will push you into a state of disorder and you will be unable to focus on the new you.

- When you're in the high-range Beta state, your focus is on the Big three and it is impossible for you to learn because your emotions are too active and busy for your mind to function properly. In this state, your thoughts are too scattered to produce any progressive thought. Your focus will be more on one of the Big Three depending on what you're worrying about. Your thoughts are incoherent and only with a coherent brain (which comes via meditation) can you be ready for your new life.

Lessons

- When you meditate, you get to know yourself by observing and developing yourself.

- You are different from your old self when you identify things that about you that made up your old self.

- When meditating, you need to remind yourself of what you no longer want to be till your nerve cells are unwired and unfired from these thoughts and it no longer sends signals to the same genes.

- If you don't step out of your past, you can't step into your future.

- To create your new mind means that you cultivate a new mind (like a farmer does to a garden) from the scratch.

- Change requires that you unlearn the unnecessary and learn what is new and good for you.

- When you're addicted to the Big Three, you'll constantly be stressed.

- You can't look inward to your inner self when all your concentration is focused on the material world. The Big Three makes your focus range slim so you can't concentrate on anything else.

- To get the best out of meditation, try to meditate when you wake up before you get into the hustle-bustle of the day or late in the evening when you're in a relaxed state.

Goals

- To understand meditation and its benefits
- To choose a meditative technique
- To stop living subconsciously
- To meditate
- To observe the difference between your old self and your new one
- To develop observation and focus skills.

Action plans

- Understanding meditation and the gains that come with it.
- Choosing a meditative technique
- Living subconsciously
- Meditating
- Staying observant and differentiating between your old self and new self
- Developing observation skills

Questions

1. How can meditation be used to effect change?
2. What happens when meditation is used as a tool for change?
3. What are the three types of Beta waves and what makes them different?
4. In which of the Beta waves do you need to focus more on the Big Three?

5. How do you know if you're in a Beta waves state?

6. What happens to your mind when you meditate?

PART III: STEPPING TOWARD YOUR NEW DESTINY

CHAPTER NINE: THE MEDITATIVE PROCESS: INTRODUCTION AND PREPARATION

Summary

To effect the change you want and be the new person you desire to be, it has to begin from within. When you meditate, the things going on internally are the focus, not the externalities.

When you follow the meditative process that leads to change, you need to remind yourself of the goal which is to take steps to change your habits and thought process so you can have the new mind that works for the new you. By thoroughly following the processes you learn from this chapter, you'll get lost in your consciousness, step out of what defines your old reality and be free of the old habits, feelings, and thoughts.

No true change comes easy and the steps in this chapter may seem somewhat odd. You may hear yourself saying these steps or processes can't work. Don't fret, your mind and body are only reacting to change, and you need to be patient. You need to be ready to commit yourself to it.

Key takeaways from this chapter

- When you meditate, the goal is to shift your focus from your body, your environment and how time passes so that what you desire, and the thoughts running through your mind take the center stage of your mind.

- Your mind is a busy analyst but when you meditate, you go beyond the analytical mind to the subconscious mind which is where all the habits, attitudes, and behaviors that need to change reside.

- When you are ready to put into practice what you've learned, you need to follow the specific steps slated out for you. These steps only make it easier for you to follow through so that your mind doesn't get lost when you see the long list of steps. You'll see that this is just to make the skill a habit for you when you repeat it.

- To measure how well you're inculcating the changes in this chapter and this book generally, you'll see that the many steps listed for you have become a single-stringed action.

- The four-week program to practice.

o Week 1: Induction (step 1)

o Week 2: Practice induction again (step 1)

  Recognizing (step 2)

  Admitting and declaring (step 3)

  Surrendering (step 4)

o Week 3: Repeat steps 1-4

  Observing and reminding (step 5)

  Redirecting (step 6)

o Week 4: Repeat steps 1-6

  Creating and rehearsing (step 7)

- How to prepare your tools

- By writing: you need to read some description for the steps which is followed by some questions and prompts. You'll need to answer the questions provided, and you need a writing pad for that. The things you write will help you navigate through the meditative procedures through which you gain access to the operating system of your subconscious mind.

- By listening: you listen to the recorded guided sessions of meditation.

- Preparing your environment

- Location: you must find the right location to meditate. It must be a place where you can conquer the distractions that come with the environment (one of the Big Three). You must prevent distractions from this place even if it means putting up a sign to prevent people or pets. Remember to turn off your phone or do away with anything that is distracting by not bringing it to the location. If you want to play music, play soothing or relaxing music not your playlist. You can use your earphones or earplugs when you are not listening to music.

- Preparing your body

- Posture: maintain a proper posture. Lying down in a very relaxed manner can induce sleep. It's best to sit upright in a normal chair, not a rocking chair, without crossing your limbs. If you feel more comfortable crossing your legs, opt for the Indian style.

- Preventing other distractions: other distractions to the body should be avoided. This means you should wear loose clothes, avoid staying in a place that's too hot or cold, avoid wearing your wristwatch, keep drinking water within your reach, and don't drink too much water.

o Nodding of the head: if you notice you're swaying your head, you're moving into the Alpha and Theta brain wave. It will stop later and with constant practice, this wouldn't lead to falling asleep.

- Making time to meditate

o Choosing a time: when you wake up and before you sleep is a good time. It's advisable you choose a particular time for this.

o Duration: begin with your 10-20 minutes induction and as you progress from one step to another, increase the duration by 10 to 15 minutes. If you need to sleep early so you wake up early enough for this, please do.

- Preparing your mind

  o Taking control of your ego: settle down in your mind and calm every analytical thought.

o Master your body: if you constantly want to move around, focus your mind on somewhere you want to go in the future or a person you've shared a previous emotional experience with so you can calm down in your mind.

Lessons

- Any true change begins from within.
- Repetition of a new skill helps you memorize it till it becomes a habit and automatic.
- To prepare for a new experience, you must first gain the right amount of knowledge you need.

Goals

- To use the meditative process to initiate your new life and reality.

- To get lost in your consciousness.

- To step out of your known reality

- To be free of old habits, feelings, and thoughts

- To define the new you

- To gain precision, calmness, order, and creativity.

- To memorize what you learn.

- To learn meditation as a step-by-step process

Action plans

- Using the meditative process to start your new reality and life.

- Losing yourself in your consciousness

- Stepping away from your known reality

- Becoming free from old habits, thoughts, and feelings

- Defining the new you

- Gaining precision, calmness, order, and creativity.

- Memorizing what you learn

- Learning the step-by-step process of meditation

Questions

1. Why is it important to concentrate on the things you're learning?

2. How can you prepare for what you're learning?

CHAPTER TEN: OPEN THE DOOR TO YOUR CREATIVE STATE (WEEK ONE)

Summary

You may have learned that there are many negative things linked to hypnosis. However, it can be used to teach people how to change their brain waves. You can hypnotize yourself.

In this chapter, you'll learn the art and benefits of self-hypnosis (which is a state similar to meditation) and induction. In the previous chapter, you would have noticed that induction is the first step in the meditative process. Without it, meditation will be a big task you might not be able to complete.

Induction can either be the Water-Rising or the Body-Part technique. You can use both techniques and alternate them when you feel the need to do so. Both techniques can help you leave the Beta state and take you to the Alpha wave state.

Key takeaways from this chapter

- To hypnotize yourself or to get hypnotized means you're moving to a relaxed brain state. It is moving from a high wave Beta state into an Alpha state and then into a Theta wave state.
- Induction is important because it preps you for a comprehensible and clear brain wave state that aids meditation. It is the foundation for the meditation process you're learning in this book.
- Induction helps you to open yourself up and it opens up the locked part of you that is creative. To get the best out of the meditative process, you must be able to devote time to do this daily. The

meditation process for the next four weeks begins with twenty minutes of induction so you will need to familiarize yourself with it. Get comfortable and relax into it.

- You begin by sitting up straight and closing your eyes so you block out all forms of distraction from your senses and environment. This will help to reduce brain frequency so you can move toward an Alpha state.

- To continue with the induction process, you need to release yourself, be present, and love yourself. If you need soothing music as an aid, you can help yourself with it.

- The Body-Part Induction technique doesn't contradict the lack of attention you give to the Big Three just because it focuses on your body and environment. This technique helps you control your thoughts about your environment and body. You become aware of your body parts in space as well as the space around the body with the aid of your cerebellum which is at the center of your subconscious mind. You can access your subconscious mind without going through your thinking brain.

- Induction makes you interpret your feelings (how your body speaks to you) by putting off your analytical mind. When you interpret your feelings, you can make changes to the language of your operating system.

- When you focus on the Big-Three, your focus is narrow but with the Body-Part Induction process, you have a wide range focus because you're also focused on the space around your body and your body parts.

- The Water-Rising induction technique requires using your imagination to sense water filling a room. You can imagine the water rising as it moves to your ankle, your knees, waist, abdomen, chest, chin, your head, and then to all parts of the room.

Lessons
- Meditation and self-hypnosis are familiar.
- Your body speaks to you through your feelings.

Goals
- To master induction
- To begin your meditation process
- To practice the Body-Part Induction

Action plans
- Mastering induction
- Beginning your meditation process
- Practicing the Body-Part Induction

Questions
1. Does Body- Part Induction make you focus on the Big Three?
2. Why should you focus on the body?
3. What are the benefits of induction?
4. What is the benefit of open focus?

CHAPTER ELEVEN: PRUNE AWAY THE HABIT OF BEING YOURSELF (WEEK TWO)

Summary

In this chapter, you'll be moving to the second step in the meditative process. This includes recognizing, followed by admitting, and declaration followed by surrendering.

Your meditation process requires that you build on the previous foundation, which is induction. It is advisable that you practice step one for another week.

To begin the next step, you need to give the problem an identity. It is the same as giving a name to the problem. This way, you're not dealing with an ambiguous issue. When you give it a name then you begin to have power over it. After this, you'll progress to admitting, declaring, and surrendering.

Key takeaways from this chapter

- To move into step two, you begin with induction after which you identify the problem, then you progress to fixing the problem.

- When you are recognizing, you're having a daily life review. You can do this because you have the gear for this in your brain. It helps you to counter the prearranged patterns that have become second nature to your body and brain. it intrudes the emotions that have been memorized and the programs of the mind that have been hardwired.

- When you become wholly conscious, you can step out of the previous patterns that have conditioned your brain and body. It is only when you are still, relaxed, and patient that you will be able to pay attention and identify your old self that needs to change. You will disallow your subjective consciousness from continuing with previous attitudes and emotions it was acquainted with. This will free you from the way you've always lived your life as you can think differently because you have a changed mind and your self-centered ego is not in charge.

- With recognition, you'll see that you'll become more observant, and you are vigilant. You know the difference between your consciousness and your subconscious that oversaw your mind and body. You recognize who you were (the old you) via metacognition. Your conscious and subconscious are separate and no longer immersed and you know the difference between the two. This is a sign that you're on your way to getting your desired change.

- To review your life, you need to ask yourself pertinent questions to identify and recognize the aspects you want to change. These questions are frontal lobe questions and you need to write them down. They are questions about who you are, the kind of person you want the world to see, who you are within, the kind of feelings that well up inside you, the feelings you struggle with, the part of you that needs to improve and what you need to change about yourself.

- Think about a recurring emotion that you need to unmemorize and write it down. It can be anger, disgust, guilt, sadness, or any other.

It must be one emotion; you don't need to write many for now. Many times, one of these emotions can lead to many others. As you unmemorize it, the other emotions linked to it will also begin to dissipate. When you do this, you're telling your body to stop allowing your subconscious to be in charge. Think about how you feel when you experience that emotion and how you feel when you're overwhelmed by that feeling. Identify the area where that feeling stays within your body. Feel this emotion and don't run away from it because it is who you are. There's a state of mind that you can link with that emotion. Find out what it is and write it out.

- You need to accept what is going on within you as who you really are not what other people say about you. When you accept this, you can see your past mistakes for what they are and you can accept yourself for who you are. This allows you to be compassionate and loving and understand yourself. Write all these things out.

- You need to speak out about who you have been and the truth about yourself that you know. This helps you to stop the façade and the appearance you give about yourself. Now say the emotion that you're feeling. (saying it is the hardest part of all).

- After the previous step, you need to surrender yourself to a greater power. By yielding yourself, you give up what you believe you know and let go of your ego's control. Write out some of these things you would like to declare in your yielding statement.

Lessons
- Any problem you can't see can't be fixed.

- When you recognize, you review your life before you die and get to be reborn in the process.
- You can't yield yourself and still aim to control the outcome of events. It must be one of the two.
- It's beautiful to let nature take its course as you release yourself. This can only happen when you surrender and completely let go.

Goals

- To identify your problem
- To be truly conscious
- To observe the emotions within you and define the state of mind linked to that emotion.
- To acknowledge your true self
- To outwardly declare your self-limiting emotion
- To give yourself up to a greater power and let it take away your blocks.

Action plans

- Identifying your problem
- Becoming truly conscious
- Observing the emotions within you and defining the state of mind linked to that emotion.
- Acknowledging your true self
- Outwardly declaring your self-limiting emotion
- Giving yourself up to a greater power and let it remove any blocks.

Questions

1. Why do you need to name your problem?

2. What are the benefits of recognizing?

3. Why do you need to be truly conscious?

4. What do you stand to benefit when you surrender?

CHAPTER TWELVE: DISMANTLE THE MEMORY OF THE OLD YOU (Week Three)

Summary

Remember to begin your week three meditations by going through the previous steps. In step 5, you need to become familiar with yourself and groom yourself, so you become aware of what you didn't know about yourself.

With observing and reminding, you gain a higher awareness and you observe yourself better. When you see your old self better, you gain a better perspective of who you want to be and what you want to leave behind.

After observing and reminding, you move to redirecting. This is when you stop yourself from subconsciously taking the same destructive steps.

Key takeaways from this chapter

- Step 5 involves observing and reminding. You must observe who you used to be and tell yourself who you no longer want to be.

- Who you are neurologically is a combination of your thoughts and actions with every passing moment.

- You must be aware of your old self so that you catch it anytime it comes up. This is why you need to practice the previous steps because doing this helps you stay alert every time it tries to come up. Write out the thoughts that automatically come up when you are practicing step 2.

- Many of the actions we take unconsciously are taken to emotionally strengthen our personality and addiction to certain patterns. In some cases, we take certain actions to momentarily forget some of our memorized emotions.

- When you spot limiting unconscious behavior that you've memorized, write them down and memorize the list. When you become familiar with this list, you can identify when it is driving you so you can halt it. After doing this consistently, you know what triggers it and you stop it.

- When you stop yourself from subconsciously taking destructive habits or attitudes, you cause your nerve cells to unfire and unwire. When you catch yourself thinking those thoughts, remind yourself to change.

Lessons

- Your thoughts and actions must correlate. What you constantly remind yourself of, and what you do physically, make up who you are neurologically.

- Habits are created from addictions.

- By unmemorizing a negative emotion, you have the chance to exterminate an unconscious destructive behavior.

- Associative memories will lead to automatic reactions.

Goals

- To identify the thoughts that make up the old you and write them down.

- To practice observing and reminding

- To practice redirecting

- To identify associative memories

- To catch yourself before going unconscious

Action plans

- Identifying thoughts that make up the old you and writing them down.

- Practicing observing and reminding

- Practice redirecting

- Identifying associative memories

- Catching yourself before going unconscious

Questions

1. Write out the old limiting thoughts that come up automatically.

2. Write out the old limiting behaviors that come up automatically.

3. Why is it hard to stay conscious while you're going through change?

CHAPTER THIRTEEN: CREATE A NEW MIND FOR YOUR NEW FUTURE (Week Four)

Summary

Step 7 is about creating and rehearsing. You need to continue with the good and new things you're doing to get the desired you. If you think the steps involved in the process are too many, it's because you're yet to get acquainted with the steps. Once you are familiar with the steps, it becomes a single string of actions instead of many steps. Keep at it and you'll get your desired outcome.

You may become bored with the steps, and this is a good thing because it shows that you're beginning to get familiar with the steps and it will become natural soon. Look past your boredom into what you want to achieve.

Key takeaways from this chapter

- One of the best things you can do for yourself is to fall in love with the new you that's emerging. Love is stronger than other survival emotions.

- You must continue to give yourself the same frame of mind daily by rehearsing mentally about a new ideal of yourself till it becomes a part of you.

- Creating yourself requires using your imagination to bring your new self into existence. This will require asking yourself questions that make you use your frontal lobe and opens you to new possibilities while using your mind. This is a process of building your mind. Ask questions about the picture of your ideal self, your role models and what they did, who you want to be, what to say to yourself if you were the person you want to be, and how to remind yourself of who you want to be.

- Take the time to ponder on these questions and think about your answers before giving them. Give honest answers and think thoroughly before giving them. However, don't overthink or overanalyze them.

- The new personality that you've created will birth a new reality for you. Your reality is created from what you do, the way you think, and how you feel.

- Take the meditative process personally and make it your own. Ensure to measure what you're doing by doing some self-reflection. Look back at how far you've come and note what you need to do to improve. Think about how you're feeling, and how much change you've gone through.

Lessons
- Creativity is essential in creating a new you.
- It takes your honesty, desire, and will to help you get above the urges you feel.
- To aid your focus on your journey, you need to practice frequently, and increase your duration and intensity.

Goals
- To ensure you understand the previous steps.
- To lose your old mind and create a new one.

- To love the new you that's emerging

- To practice creating a new mind until it becomes a part of you.

- To master a new mind.

- To move into a state of being and become the ideal person you want.

Action plans

- Ensuring you understand the previous steps.

- Losing your mind and creating a new one.

- Loving the new you that's emerging.

- Practicing creating a new mind until it becomes a part of you

- Mastering a new mind

- Moving into a state of being and becoming the ideal person you want.

Questions

1. Why is it important to mentally rehearse who you want to be?

2. Why is it important to meditate to create a new you?

3. Why is your new personality important?

4. Write out your mental-rehearsal meditation for the new you that you want to create.

CHAPTER FOURTEEN: DEMONSTRATING AND BEING: LIVING YOUR NEW REALITY

Summary

When you can live out the change you've been working on, it shows that you've internally memorized an order that is stronger than an environmental hint.

Key takeaways from this chapter

- When you become a new being, your internal neurochemical state is in place and there's no stimulus in your external incoherent world that can upset who you are so your body and mind work together.

- When you demonstrate all you've learned, you're living in your new self. It is basking in the exhilaration and hope of your new life. To see the signs of the life you created, you must stay and live from the energy that created that life. You can write out notes to remind you of what you can be conscious about and place them where you can easily see them.

Lessons

- When who you are and how you appear are the same, you've broken free from the old you.

- Your life is the picture of your mind in all ways.

- You and your life are the same.

Goals

- For your environment to no longer control you

- To be ahead of your time

- To match your behavior and goal

- To expect feedback.

- To be transparent

- To experience true love

Action plans

- Your environment no longer controls you.

- Be ahead of your time.

- Matching your behavior and goal

- Expecting feedback

- Becoming transparent

- Experiencing true love

Questions

1. How can you maintain the change in your life so you don't return to your previous self?

2. How do you know if you're doing your meditation properly?

3. What's the sign of being transparent?

4. Why do you need to connect to your consciousness?

To wrap this up...

We are more than physical beings. We are multidimensional beings full of energy, we are divine beings, and we need to live from our identity because it is the only way to live a life with meaning. We have power over our lives and destiny. We can make the changes and improvements we want, and this is possible with the information you get from this book.

In between dropping everything about your old life or mind and creating a new one, you may feel like returning to the old life because change isn't as easy as we think it is. Living out of the familiar can be initially scary. This is a place of potential because it is a place of possibilities.

To find your true self, you'll need the information in this book. You open the door to your conscious energetic self and when you do, you'll find love coursing through your system. It begins with your attention which is why you must be focused and conscious. Focus on what's going on within you instead of focusing on your environment, time, and your body (the Big Three). Changing your thoughts is the beginning of finding yourself and changing your life.

Made in United States
Troutdale, OR
01/28/2024

17129875R20040